A provisional atlas of the shieldbugs and allies of Shropshire

Pete Boardman (editor)

FSC
BRINGING
ENVIRONMENTAL
UNDERSTANDING TO ALL

© Field Studies Council 2014
ISBN: 978 1 908819 12 3
SP7.

Contents

Acknowledgements

Many thanks to everyone who has helped out with this project including; all those who gave up lots of their time recording, photographing, commenting, and reviewing. Special thanks to everyone who supplied photos for this atlas – some amazing images! Thanks to all at FSC Publications for their help and Sue Townsend at FSC Head Office for supporting my drive to get the atlases off the ground. Most preparation time was done in time paid for by my Heritage Lottery Fund (HLF) project so thank you to them, my monitor Harriet Carty, and everyone who bought a lottery ticket that supports projects like ours. Thanks to Daniel Lockett at Ludlow Museum for allowing me access the Frances Pitt collection; fundamental in our early attempts to put together a Shropshire list. Thanks to the Liverpool Museum Entomology Department who freely gave access to their Shropshire reports and have inspired a number of us into entomology over the years. A big thank you also must go to the Wyre Forest Study Group for their support, for supplying records through the Worcestershire BRC. Thanks particularly to Rosemary Winnall, Brett Westwood, John & Denise Bingham, and Jane & Dave Scott. Also we must thank WFSG for inviting Gary Farmer to speak at the 2009 Worcester Entomological Day, without which this publication would never have arisen. Maps are generated using DMAP software © Dr Alan Morton. The addition of towns and major rivers are courtesy of John Arnfield (Map 1).

Introduction

It must be reasonably uncommon that the geneses of projects of this sort are able to be traced to a particular time and place but in this case we can do precisely that. For at lunchtime on Saturday 7th November 2009 the idea was born for this publication. This followed an inspirational talk by Gary Farmer to the Worcestershire entomological folk (and several Shropshire interlopers) at the annual Worcestershire Entomology Day. Those of us there from Shropshire doubted any similar illustrated talk could be currently done on Shropshire's shieldbug fauna, given the lack of a 'bug' recorder and with only a fledgling local records centre. It became apparent as Ian Thompson, Ian Cheeseborough, Caroline Uff, and I talked over sandwiches that if we wanted to remedy this situation we'd need to organise ourselves.

Fortunately at the time I was running a taxonomic training project for the Field Studies Council (FSC) and this enabled me to include shieldbug identification training in the 2010 and 2011 programme of events. Over time a mixture of seasoned Shropshire recorders and newly enthused souls, with support from myself, formed a loosely bound 'bug group' that set out to discover more and map these wonderful creatures. We met for field recording events and indoor summary events as the manifestation of the atlas looked more likely. Also the word had been spread to community groups and other recorders were made aware of our plans. Finally with a plan in place we connected with the national recorder Tristan Bantock.

The atlas is based upon just over 3000 records, the vast majority of which are from the period since Gary's talk in 2009, so I think it is fair to say that we've achieved quite a lot in a short period of time. When it came to researching historical records the evidence suggests that this group were not widely recorded in the county. Records were mined from available sources such as the surveys the Liverpool Museum entomological team carried out at a variety of sites in Shropshire, and the collections at Ludlow Museum, though frustratingly most of the specimens in the Frances Pitt collection have no site labels to demonstrate where the insects were collected. Bernard Nau (the national recorder at the inception of our project) sent me a number of record cards which I transcribed for the project and the Wyre Forest Study Group database (through the Worcester Biological Records Centre) opened up their database of Shropshire records, as well as their great knowledge and encouragement! A full list of recorders involved in the atlas is listed on page 2.

I think we must also mention the role of *Shieldbugs of Surrey* by Roger Hawkins (Hawkins 2003) which every shieldbug recorder who owns counts as an inspiration! That book was honed over a 20 year period and so understandably holds far more detailed information on the Surrey fauna than this atlas does for Shropshire. Also the excellent Surrey book, as well as the wonderful photographic guide written by Evans and Edmondson (2005), as well as the incredible British Bugs website (www.british-bugs.org.uk), preclude the need for this book to go into any great detail on species identification by means of dichotomous keys etc. If keys are required however, they can be found in both the Surrey book and also in the excellent account of Southampton's Shieldbugs (SNHS, 2007) which is currently available as a download on the internet. Further to this at family level the AIDGAP *Key to families of British Bugs* (Unwin, 2001) published by the Field Studies Council is still available from FSC Publications.

It is assumed that these resources are freely available and accessible to everyone. The species accounts in this book therefore are not long prescriptions of how to identify the insect but are relayed in a narrative style made up of anecdotes from the recorders and in some cases the history of how we came to know what we know about the species in our county. There is also a quick 'Ease of identification score' plus 'an ease of finding score' as some species are easy to identify but take a lot of finding. The great asset of any natural historian or entomologist is after all the ability of 'how to look' and I hope we can translate that from the anecdotes we relate! We hope that this information is particularly useful for the shieldbug student and wherever possible we explain habitat, microclimate, plant associations, and any snippets that may be of interest.

This atlas is one of a number to be published examining the distribution of some of Shropshire's invertebrate groups including craneflies, micro-moths, long-horned beetles, and bees, wasps, and ants. The atlases follow an upsurge in entomological interest in Shropshire that has in some way been encouraged by the Invertebrate Challenge Project, funded by the Heritage Lottery Fund (HLF). This funding has enabled some of my time to be spent in the pursuit of these publications and the species that inhabit them, for which I am truly grateful. Hopefully they will inspire a continuing interest in Shropshire's rich invertebrate fauna.

Pete Boardman (Editor).

Recorders

This list represents everyone who has submitted records to this atlas. People who have submitted over fifty records, or recorders who went out of their way to visit unrecorded tetrads specifically for shieldbugs, are noted in **bold type**.

Keith Alexander, Mike Ashton, Jess Balai, John Balcombe, Tristan Bantock, Martin Barrett, **Denise and John Bingham, Godfrey Blunt**, **Karen and Peter Boardman,** Morgan and Paul Bowers, Sheila Brooke, **Amanda Brown and Glen Forde**, Rich Burkmar, Steve Butler, **Nigel Cane-Honeysett,** Bex Cartwright, **Ian Cheeseborough,** Harriet Carty, Alec Connah, C. Cooke, Mike Coutts (deceased), **Jim Cresswell, Allan Dawes,** David Denman, John Dodgson, Mark Duffell, **Clive and Jacki Dyer, Stuart Edmunds,** Mike Fallon, Fred Fincher (deceased), Clare Flynn, Lisa Foster, **Keith Fowler, Michelle Furber and Warren Putter**, Steve Gill, Rhona Goddard, Harry Green, Francesca Griffith, Dave Grundy, Dale Harrison, Heather Hathaway, Roger D. Hawkins, **Sue, Gwyn and Steve Hiatt,** Pete Hicks, K. Hodgkiss, J.A. Hollier, Heather Hopkinson, Les Hughes, Tony Jacques, S.E. Jaggs, Annabel Johncock, Adrian Jones, **Nigel Jones**, Steve Judd, **Maria Justamond**, Bob Kemp, Peter Kirby, S.J. Lambert, Pete Lambert, Steve Lane, Gordon Leel, **Liverpool Museum Entomology Department**, Kirsten Lord, Matt Marston, John Mason, Kevin McGee, Don McNeil, J.W. Meiklejohn, Ken and Rita Merrifield, **Jay Mitchell, Margaret and Stephen Mitchell**, Bernard S. Nau, P. Nicholson, John Norton (deceased), Matthew Oates, John Partridge, Lyn Petre, Colin W. Plant, David Poynton, Will Prestwood, Alex Rogers, Glenn Rostron, Rothamsted Insect Survey, Edward Sopp, Strettons Area Community Wildlife Group, Mike Samworth, P. Saunders, Dave and Jane Scott, SGCT volunteer recorders, **Anne and Jim Shaw**, David Sheppard, Melissa Short, Jo and Mike Shurmer, **Shropshire Invertebrates Group**, Peter Skidmore (deceased), Mike S. Smith, David Smith, South Staffordshire Naturalists' Society, Graham Statham, **Sue Swindells**, Peter Tarrant, **Jo and Ian Thompson**, Clare Toner, Sue Townsend, Harriet Trower, **Caroline Uff**, Mrs Uttley, **Paul E. Watts**, William Watkins, Graham Wenman, Brett Westwood, **Wyre Forest Study Group**, **Wrekin Forest Volunteers**, Sarah Whild, **David Williams**, Rosemary Winnall, Kat Woods, Dan Wrench, Jonathan J. Wright, Liz Wright, Richard Wright, Penny Wysome, Simon Yates.

Shieldbug and allies anatomy – parts mentioned in the text

We've tried to keep this atlas as non-technical as possible however the following parts are referred to in the text. Shieldbugs and allies have two pairs of wings, the forewings being hardened for most of their length and providing protection for the hindwings underneath.

pronotum

scutellum

ocelli

tibia

connexivum

tarsal segments

Figure 1. Main features of shieldbug anatomy. Photo: David Williams.

Figure 2. Forest Bug revealing hindwings. Photo: Jim Shaw.

Rhopalid bugs and other allies however have degrees of hardening on the forewing but very much reduced when compared to shieldbugs.

Figure 3. Rhopalid bug forewing. Photo: Pete Boardman.

Shieldbug and allies lifecycle

Putting philosophical arguments to one side, the shieldbug lifecycle starts as an egg, usually grouped into divisions of seven (seven, fourteen, twenty one, etc). The eggs hatch and the larvae progress through five nymphal stages (or instars) before reaching adulthood. These stages can look similar to the adult they will become or completely different depending upon species. Illustrations of the various instars can be found readily on the British Bugs website, although we have included an example of each instar across a number of species below. When the final instar nymph makes the transition to adulthood the early adult takes a little while to adopt the full colouration and is said to be at a teneral stage. Finally some of the species that overwinter as adults will change colouration, adopting less bright colours to help them become less conspicuous. A few examples are shown below:

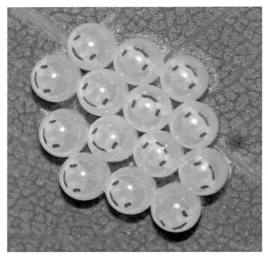

Figure 4. Eggs of Forest Bug. Photo: David Williams.

Figure 5. First instar Green Shieldbug.
Photo: Maria Justamond.

Figure 6. Second instar Parent. Photo: Maria Justamond.

Figure 7. Third instar Hawthorn Shieldbug.
Photo: Pete Boardman.

Figure 8. Fourth instar Green Shieldbug.
Photo: Pete Boardman.

Figure 9. Final instar Bronze Shieldbug.
Photo: Pete Boardman.

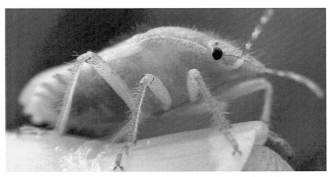

Figure 10. Teneral Bronze Shieldbug.
Photo: Pete Boardman.

Figure 11. Teneral Sloe Bug. Note hairs on pronutum and head.
Photo: Maria Justamond.

Figure 13. Parent Bug in winter
colouration. Photo: Jim Cresswell.

Figure 12. Green Shieldbug in winter colouration.
Photo: Maria Justamond.

The story of the misplaced scutellum

During 2010 I organised and co-led a number of training events that looked at shieldbug identification and doubled as field days. These enabled both new and old hands to come along and make a contribution to the early atlas maps and help those new to the process acquaint themselves with some of the modern Shropshire names of entomology. These days always seemed popular and it was great, as it always is, to see people learn in the field, which is after all the raison d'être for the Field Studies Council and externally funded projects like mine.

Following one such event we had a visit by the funders who wanted to see first hand the events we ran, and I suppose, to make sure that everything they were funding was being run appropriately, and how we'd proposed to run it. So at the next event (as it turned out it was a non-entomological event) the monitor from the funders came out with us. One shieldbug group member, who shall remain nameless, (and who we'll call 'Mr X' to save his blushes), was also on this event and was very keen to demonstrate his new found knowledge to the monitor when we happened across a shieldbug in Benthall Edge Wood at Ironbridge. I stood to his side whilst he relayed his new found knowledge.

Mr X: 'Have you seen this shieldbug? It's a Forest Bug, sometimes called a Red-legged Shieldbug, but the legs can be quite variable in colour.'

Monitor: 'No, wow – that's fabulous! Where did you find that, and how did you know what it was?'

Mr X: 'I've been on a few training days with Pete recently and also see them at home in the garden. They are predatory bugs so could turn up anywhere on vegetation but you often see them on trees.'

Monitor: 'Wow, that's great! What a spectacular bug!'

Mr X: 'Do you know why they are called shieldbugs?'

Monitor: 'No.'

Mr X: 'Well if you look at the general shape of the insect it looks really shield-shaped, particularly this family, but also the general name comes from this feature here at the back of the pronotum (pointing to illustrate), it's a triangular shield-shaped feature, and it's called the scrotum.'

Monitor: (jaw drops open)

Me: (low whispered moan with some exasperation) 'Scutellum!!!!'

Mr X: 'Sorry, yes, scutellum from the Latin for shield.'

Thankfully we soon moved on and nothing more was said about the shieldbug 'scrotum'. The funders thankfully continue to fund us.

Checklist of species recorded in Shropshire

Pentatomoidea – shieldbugs

Acanthosomatidae
Acanthosoma haemorrhoidale (Linnaeus, 1758) Hawthorn Shieldbug
Cyphostethus tristiatus (Fabricius, 1787) Juniper Shieldbug
Elasmostethus interstinctus (Linnaeus, 1758) Birch Shieldbug
Elasmuchea grisea (Linnaeus, 1758) Parent Bug

Scutelleridae
Eurygaster testudinaria (Geoffrey, 1785) Tortoise Bug

Cydnidae
Legnotus limbosus (Geoffrey, 1785) Bordered Shieldbug
Tritomegas bicolor (Linnaeus, 1758) Pied Shieldbug
Sehirus biguttatus (Linnaeus, 1758) Cow-wheat Shieldbug
Sehirus luctuosus Mulsant and Rey, 1886 Forget-me-not Shieldbug

Pentatomidae
Graphosoma lineatum (Linnaeus, 1758) Striped Shieldbug **VAGRANT**
Aelia acuminata (Linnaeus, 1758) Bishop's Mitre Shieldbug
Neottiglossa pusilla (Gmelin, 1789) Small Grass Shieldbug
Eysarcoris venustissimus (Schrank, 1776) Woundwort Shieldbug
Palomena prasina (Linnaeus, 1761) Green Shieldbug
Dolycoris baccarum (Linnaeus, 1758) Sloe Bug
Piezodorus lituratus (Fabricius, 1789) Gorse Shieldbug
Pentatoma rufipes (Linnaeus, 1758) Forest Bug
Eurydema oleracea (Linnaeus, 1758) Brassica Bug
Picromerus bidens (Linnaeus, 1758) Spiked Shieldbug
Troilus luridus (Fabricius, 1775) Bronze Shieldbug
Rhacognathus punctatus (Linnaeus, 1758) Heather Shieldbug
Zicrona caerulea (Linnaeus, 1758) Blue Bug

Coreoidea – squashbugs, scentless plant bugs, spurge bugs

Coreidae
Coreus marginatus (Linnaeus, 1758) Dock Bug
Coriomeris denticulatus (Scopoli, 1763) Denticulate Leatherbug
Leptoglossus occidentalis (Heidemann, 1910) Western Conifer Seedbug **VAGRANT**

Rhopalidae
Corizus hyoscyami (Linnaeus, 1758)
Rhopalus subrufus (Gmelin, 1788)
Myrmus miriformis (Fallén, 1807)
Stictopleurus abutilon (Rossi, 1790)

Stenocephalidae
Dicranocephalus medius (Mulsant and Rey, 1870)

Geography, geology and species movement

The complex and fascinating geology of Shropshire is the subject of many books and is summarised in the map below (Map 2). In terms of the importance of specific geological conditions most shieldbugs are not overly affected, however those that are have been dealt with individually within the species accounts. Probably more important a factor to a number of shieldbugs is the ability of the soils on which they live to be free-draining and therefore to warm up quickly. This is certainly important for species such as the pied shieldbug which is associated with plants such as white-dead nettle. Whilst this plant is not particularly restricted by geology or hydrological conditions, the shieldbug is only found where soils are free-draining; be they on sandy, limestone, or neutral soils. Micro-climate is also an important factor and the experienced shieldbug watcher quickly becomes aware of where the more sheltered, or south-facing aspects are within habitats.

One very important thing to consider in terms of geography and shieldbugs in Shropshire is the role of the River Severn corridor in the spread of shieldbugs through the county. The River Severn enters the county from the south-east by the

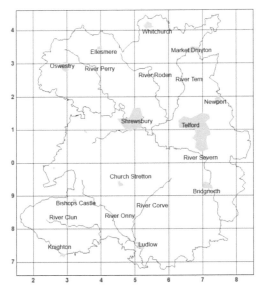

Map 1. Shropshire map used for species dot maps.

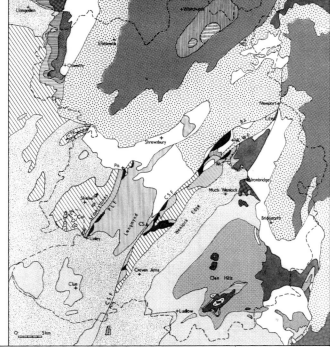

Map 2. Geological map of Shropshire.

Wyre Forest and its course heads in a north-westerly direction flowing through Ironbridge, Shrewsbury and beyond. Its southern stretches pass through well-drained low-lying fossilised sands of the Permian Sandstone with a warmer microclimate than the surrounding land to the west making ideal conditions for shieldbugs at sites like Dudmaston and Alveley. So perhaps not unsurprisingly this route into the county is the main one used by not just shieldbugs but most invertebrates that spread into the county from the south. Compare this to south-western Shropshire. The Clun uplands tend to be cooler, and are mostly made up of improved sheep-grazed pastures and coniferous forestry. To the north are the upland moorlands of the Long Mynd, where the higher elevation routinely delays insect phenology by two or more weeks compared to the sheltered lowlands. Any insects that do enter the county from the south-west are likely to use the river valleys of the Clun, the Onny and the Corve.

If one looks at the map (Map 3) with a squint one can just about see the relationship between the course of the River Severn and the most well recorded tetrads (darker colours). The other obvious conclusion that can be made is that much of the south-west of the county has yet to be visited for shieldbug recording, but I would suggest it would be unlikely that many sites in this part of the county would produce more than a few mobile species, particularly in the uplands, as very few Shropshire species are adapted to colder and wetter conditions.

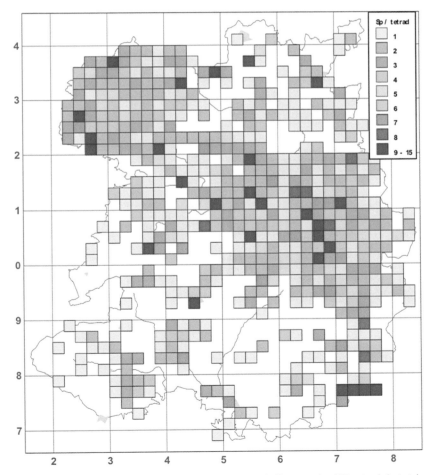

Map 3. Coincidence map of all Shropshire shieldbugs and allies covering 553 tetrads in total.

Notes on the maps and species accounts

The species accounts and maps within this book are based upon approximately 3000 records from 553 tetrads. There are still plenty of tetrads within Shropshire that have not been recorded at all (870 whole tetrads). Maps at this stage probably reflect recording effort but are a start to a greater understanding of species distribution. They do at least give us the opportunity to start to see the true distribution of the 30 species that have been found within Shropshire. It is hoped that further work will continue to update these maps until eventually at least one species has been recorded from every tetrad. If time, money, and volunteer effort were limitless we could perhaps expect a 'par' score for every tetrad but we are not at, or anywhere near, that stage yet so that is perhaps something that could be taken up by a second edition of this atlas.

Note about the Wyre Forest. Several species accounts illustrate the importance of the Wyre Forest for a number of shieldbug and allied species. It should be noted that only a limited part of the Forest is within Shropshire (VC40) with the majority sitting within Worcestershire (VC37) and some also within Staffordshire (VC39). Wherever the Wyre Forest is mentioned in the text we refer to the part of the Forest within Shropshire only.

Most commonly encountered Shropshire species

The table below (Table 1) illustrates the most commonly encountered species recorded to date in Shropshire listing how many tetrads (2km x 2km squares) each species has been recorded from. Shropshire has 870 whole tetrads in total rising to 925 if the 'fiddly bits' around the edge are counted.

Species	No. of tetrads (2 km x 2 km squares) recorded in	Species	No. of tetrads (2 km x 2 km squares) recorded in
Green Shieldbug	372	*Corizus hyoscyami*	15
Hawthorn Shieldbug	186	Bishop's Mitre Shieldbug	13
Sloe Shieldbug	145	Small Grass Shieldbug	11
Forest Shieldbug	117	Forget-me-not Shieldbug	11
Birch Shieldbug	114	*Myrmus miriformis*	8
Dock Bug	110	Denticulate Leatherbug	4
Woundwort Shieldbug	85	Heather Shieldbug	4
Bronze Shieldbug	73	Bordered Shieldbug	4
Gorse Shieldbug	65	Tortoise Shieldbug	3
Parent Shieldbug	60	*Dicranocephalus medius*	3
Pied Shieldbug	56	Cow-wheat Shieldbug	2
Spiked Shieldbug	39	Western Conifer Seedbug	2
Juniper Shieldbug	24	Brassica Shieldbug	1
Blue Shieldbug	22	*Stictopleurus abutilon*	1
Rhopalus subrufus	20	Striped Shieldbug	1

Table 1. The most commonly encountered Shropshire species.

Ease of identification and ease of finding

The identification of shieldbugs and allies is straightforward for the majority of adults of those species that are found in Shropshire, and to some extent with ease for a number of instars and even the eggs of some species. Although this Atlas does not go into great detail on the identification of species, we thought it would be useful to have a quick gauge of ease of identification alongside a gauge of how easy they are to find (see Table 2). Both have a 1-5 scale where 1 is easy to identify as an adult and 5 is difficult where a specimen may need to be taken or a very detailed photograph showing a key feature. Likewise with ease of finding, 1 is easy to find and 5 is difficult needing specialist techniques such as sieving or sifting leaf litter.

Ease of identification (adults)		Ease of finding (adults)	
1	Very easy to identify as adult. No species to cause confusion within Shropshire.	1	Likely to be found very easily in vegetated places
2	Easy to identify. Maybe a lookalike species that is similar but easily resolved.	2	Sometimes targeting needed i.e. specific plant species association but generally easily found
3	Tricky to identify but soon resolved. Maybe several lookalike species or confusion with other orders of insects	3	Targeting most likely needed to find species or most likely that a sweep net is needed to find the species.
4	Tricky to identify without reference to field guide etc unless prior knowledge. The County Recorder is probably going to ask to see specimen or photograph if recorded by a beginner.	4	Even with targeting, and associated plant species and geological knowledge, only occasionally found, and perhaps restricted distribution in the county.
5	Specimen needed for examination of microscopic features or very good photo that shows specific anatomical feature. The County Recorder will probably not accept record based on field sighting alone.	5	Very difficult to find without the use of special techniques (sieving vegetation litter etc), and probably of very limited distribution in the county.

Table 2. Ease of identification and ease of finding ratings explained.

Recording shieldbugs and allies in Shropshire

When the process started of putting together and evaluating records, Shropshire VC40 did not have a County Recorder of Hemiptera that could be called on for information or indeed for records. Thankfully that situation has now changed. We encourage people to continue to send us records of shieldbugs and allies to build on the maps in this Atlas.

Please send your records to;

Mr. Keith Fowler – email: keith.c.fowler@blueyonder.co.uk

Species accounts of shieldbugs and allies found in Shropshire

Acanthosomatidae – the keeled shieldbugs

There are four UK species, all of which are found in Shropshire. These bugs have a large keel on the underside of the thorax, and the tarsi have two segments. A key to shieldbugs and allied insects can be found in Hawkins (2003) (p28-45).

Acanthosoma haemorrhoidale
(Linnaeus, 1758) Hawthorn Shieldbug

GB distribution and status: Common throughout England and parts of Wales and Scotland.
Ease of identification: 1
Ease of finding: 2

This is a ubiquitous and easily identified species found commonly throughout the county where hawthorn trees and hedgerows containing hawthorn and other plants are located. In Shropshire it has also been recorded on holly, bramble, whitebeam, nettle, wych elm, mulberry and a range of other plants, as well as being found in leaf litter on the ground on a couple of occasions. Maria Justamond found an instar on whitebeam in Wellington and indeed whitebeam was one of a number of plants that the Surrey survey recorded as foodplants of the species (Hawkins 2003).

It has regularly been found at moth trap light by Anne and Jim Shaw in their Newport garden, and was found by Caroline Uff in a dormouse box on Wenlock Edge. I saved one from certain death by retrieving it as it was floating in a cattle water trough at Preston Montford, though my expected Daily Mirror Pride of Britain award nomination failed to arrive.

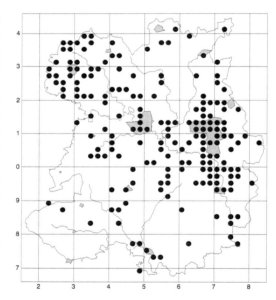

Map 4. Distribution (2km) of *Acanthosoma haemorrhoidale*.

It has been recorded in nearly every month of the year in Shropshire but the records suggest it is more frequently encountered during late summer when the hawthorn bushes are bearing their berries. Hedgerows and trees with berries, particularly where sheltered and in south-facing sunshine, are often good places to look.

Figure 14. Hawthorn Shieldbug. Photo: David Williams.

Figure 15. Final instar nymph. Photo: Pete Boardman.

Figure 16. Third instar nymph. Photo: Maria Justamond.

Cyphostethus tristiatus
(Fabricius, 1787) Juniper Shieldbug

GB distribution and status: Common through eastern and central England. Restricted distribution in Wales and decreasing from Cumbria northwards with few Scottish records.

Ease of identification: 1

Ease of finding: 3

When putting together our original list of what we might expect to find in Shropshire this species was one we assumed would have turned up, particularly at moth trap light given the number of garden moth traps running in the county, but it seemed unexpectedly absent. Tristan Bantock confirmed that we should be seeing this insect and advised us to look on Lawson's cypress or other cultivars of cypress that occur in gardens, churchyards and parks. Unbelievably that same week Keith Fowler came across one in Kemberton Churchyard on a very snowy February morning (Fowler, 2012) and Maria Justamond encountered one a couple of weeks later at Upton Magna (both February 2012 records). After that a number of sightings were made once recorders had been made aware of where and how to look. Sue Swindells counted forty-seven adults and nymphs on a cypress tree at Rhewl, near Oswestry, whilst Maria Justamond found them in

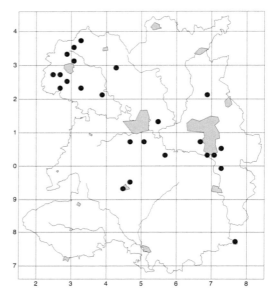

Map 5. Distribution (2km) of *Cyphostethus tristiatus.*

similarly large numbers on the cypress trees within the Oswestry Showground. It was with a little surprise that when the Worcestershire data arrived recently we noted that entomologist Keith Alexander discovered the bug in the Wyre Forest in 1984! Therefore it seems that our excitement in 2012 was only twenty eight years out of date!

The distribution of this species does seem a little odd as it is one that has spread from the south but the majority of records are in the north west of Shropshire around Oswestry. The distribution map does perhaps suggest the spread up the River Severn corridor method of entering Shropshire. This could be down to the location of suitable amounts of cypress, or simply accidental fieldwork bias. It does seem surprising though that so few records have been made in southern Shropshire where suitable habitat is located. I've failed to find them on cypresses around Bridgnorth but am not aware of any other failures to locate them in the south so it may be too early to truly know the distribution pattern of this species.

Interestingly Godfrey Blunt reports that two micro-moths have recently been found on cypress. These are *Argyresthia trifasciata* Staudinger, 1871 (first Shropshire record 2012) and *Argyresthia cupressella* Walsingham, 1890 (first Shropshire record 2013) (Blunt *in prep*). Both are extending their British ranges northwards and westwards using cypress as their main foodplant. Is this the case with the Juniper Shieldbug or have they been here all along and we haven't seen them until we made a proper effort to look?

Although all Shropshire records to date have been associated with species of cypress, other coniferous trees, notably Norway spruce, western red cedar and Douglas fir, have been mentioned by Hawkins (2003) as potential overwintering sites.

Figure 17. Adult Juniper Shieldbug. Photo: Maria Justamond.

Figure 18. Mid-instar nymph. Photo: Maria Justamond.

Figure 19. Adult Juniper Shieldbug. Photo: David Williams.

Elasmostethus interstinctus
(Linnaeus, 1758) Birch Shieldbug

GB distribution and status: Common throughout with the exception of the south-western England.

Ease of identification: 2

Ease of finding: 2

This is a very common and widespread shieldbug which is found throughout Shropshire. It is at first glance potentially mistaken for a smaller version of the Hawthorn Shieldbug or the similar sized Parent Shieldbug. Separation from the latter is easily done via a comparison of the colour of the top of the scutellum (red in the Birch Shieldbug whilst the Parent bears a black patch) and the connexivum of the Parent is striped whereas that of the Birch is not.

It is mostly often found on birch trees but it has been recorded on nettle, rowan, holly, and ivy. It has also been found walking on leaf litter and was the most frequently recorded shieldbug at Dave Grundy's moth trap sessions on Bettisfield Moss during 2013.

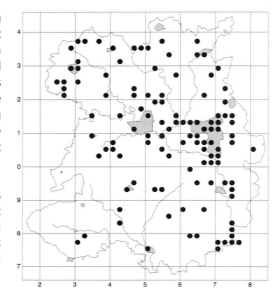

Map 6. Distribution (2km) of *Elasmostethus interstinctus.*

The best place to look for adults and nymphs is on birches with ripening catkins. It is probably one of the 'par' species that should turn up in pretty much every tetrad given the ubiquity of birch trees. Sadly no one seems to get overly excited about it and you never hear entomologists exclaim 'Oh wow it's a sunny day, let's go out and look for Birch Shieldbugs!' Consequently when I was asking for anecdotes about Shropshire species for these species accounts nobody returned any about this species. The nearest I can provide was when I was due to catch a train from Ludlow railway station and I parked my car in the small car park there and thought 'oh a birch with lots of ripe catkins' and sure enough, a ten second glance was all that was needed to confirm my suspicion. Not much of an anecdote, but the best we can do from Shropshire.

[Ed – following the circulation of this account as a draft text I received this anecdote from Keith Fowler. 'Early in the year I visited Granville (Country Park) to carry out a hedgerow survey and as a side-line attacked every Birch I could find but found no shieldbugs. At the end of the survey we passed the new housing there and noted a couple of young birches had been planted to help "beautify" the area. Resignedly I tapped one of them with my net and out fell five Birch Shieldbugs!']

Figure 20. Birch Shieldbug. Photo: Pete Boardman.

Figure 21. 5th instar nymph. Photo: Jim Cresswell.

Figure 22. Variety of instars. Photo: Clive Dyer.

Elasmuchea grisea
(Linnaeus, 1758) Parent Bug

GB distribution and status: Common throughout.

Ease of identification: 2

Ease of finding: 2

The distribution of this species is very similar to the Birch Shieldbug, and as both species use the same tree species, and are often on the same trees, that is not surprising. Apart from the differences in appearance (discussed under the previous species) there is an obvious difference in the behaviour as the female of this species assumes parental responsibility. Later larval instars are easily recognised by the black vertical stripes on the head and pronotum.

During 2013 Maria Justamond followed the progress of a particular Parent Bug and 'adopted it' on her local patch at Shawbury Heath (heathy woodland, part of which has been felled of conifers in recent years). Her field notes are as follows.

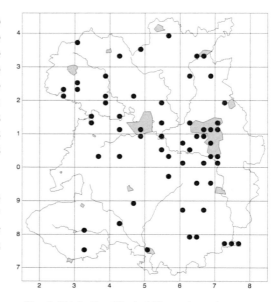

Map 7. Distribution (2km) of *Elasmuchea grisea.*

06.06.13 – First spotted the Parent Bugs in cop on a silver birch catkin.

17.06.13 – Checked back regularly and finally found female on eggs on back of birch leaf. (Parent Bug 'mum' was very good at her job as the whole time she was with the eggs, and then larvae. She made it difficult for me to take photos as she'd lean towards the lens to protect them!)

01.07.13 – More regular checks, and managed to find eggs just hatching out!

08.07.13 – Nymphs are starting to get their characteristic stripes, still all on the back of the same leaf.

11.07.13 – Just three days later, 'mum' has taken them up to a catkin to feed. (It took me a while to find them!)

14.07.13 – Still on same catkin and now two weeks old, but no sign of mum, so assume her job was done and she had died? [Ed: Hawkins (2009) note that some authors have also noted the female dies whilst tending their brood]

17.07.13 – Two and a half weeks old and the stripes are much bolder.

21.07.13 – Three weeks old and the nymphs are moving around more but still in close proximity to one another.

25.07.13 – Three and a half weeks, the nymphs are harder still to find as more spread out. Some further up the tree, just about reachable. Have their gorgeous stripy markings now.

Figure 24. Final instar nymphs. Photo: Clive Dyer.

Figure 23. Adult female parenting eggs.
Photo: David Williams.

Figure 25. Adult. Photo: Maria Justamond.

Scutelleridae – the tortoise bugs

There are four UK species with only one species occurring in Shropshire. The scutellums of these bugs reach the end of the abdomen and the tarsi have three segments.

Eurygaster testudinaria
(Geoffrey, 1785) Tortoise Bug

GB distribution and status: Common in southern England and southern parts of Wales. Rare elsewhere.

Ease of identification: 2

Ease of finding: 3

This relatively large and obvious bug ranges from light brown to dark brown with additional purple markings (see John Bingham's photos) so some confusion may occur initially if unfamiliar with the species.

This was another shieldbug where upon compiling the original county list we had the frustration of a Frances Pitt specimen in Ludlow Museum but no proof to link it to Shropshire. All current records in Shropshire are from the Wyre Forest with 2011 the first year of discovery on the Shropshire side of the Forest. This leads to the question – was the Tortoise Bug a Shropshire species that disappeared and re-emerged as part of the known recent surge northwards of this species? Rosemary Winnall reports that all the specimens she has encountered have been swept from damp grassland, either alongside Dowles Brook (which marks the Shropshire / Worcestershire boundary), one of its tributaries, or on one of the several wet flushes in the area. It is also known from drier grasslands elsewhere in the country but has of yet not been found in drier grasslands of Shropshire.

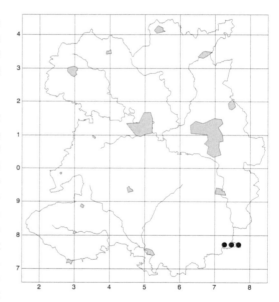

Map 8. Distribution (2km) of *Eurygaster testudinaria*.

Figure 26. Dark colour-form. Photo: John Bingham.

Figure 27. Light colour-form. Photo: John Bingham.

Figure 28. Final instar. Photo: John Bingham.

Cydnidae – the burrowing bugs

There are eight species of burrowing bug in the UK and four of them occur in our county. They are all generally small black bugs with spines on their tibiae that they use for burrowing into the ground. This family have tarsi with three segments.

Legnotus limbosus
(Geoffrey, 1785) Bordered Shieldbug

GB distribution and status: Southern and central England up to the Humber. Uncommon in Wales.
Ease of identification: 4
Ease of finding: 4

This is a tiny shieldbug that without doubt must be one of the most easily overlooked as it is only around 4 mm in size. We were first alerted to its potential presence in Shropshire by a specimen in the Frances Pitt collection at Ludlow Museum. Sadly no data label was on the specimen but given Frances lived close to Bridgnorth most of her life and was known to explore the local area and collect insects, it was likely this was a Shropshire insect. Consultation of the species map on the NBN Gateway (data.nbn.org.uk) showed existing records just to the south of us and so easily be something to look out for. Although the insect is known to be allied to bedstraws, as the Surrey atlas points out, despite it being recorded in 25 tetrads in Surrey there were no observations of feeding activity. Indeed most records were made away from bedstraw plants (Hawkins, 2003).

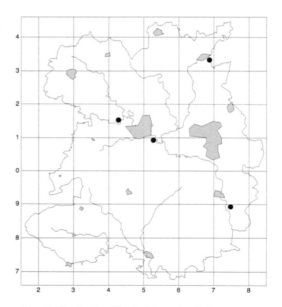

Map 9. Distribution (2km) of *Legnotus limbosus*.

Our first break came on a shieldbug and cranefly recording trip to the Market Drayton area on a wet day in mid May 2012. A bedraggled Don McNeil returned from sweeping a large stand of ruderal vegetation (including cleavers) at Tyrley Locks with a sodden sweep net and a specimen of the shieldbug. The second record came on the first warm, sunny day of 2012 (apparently 22 May!) and was seen courtesy of Caroline Uff, sat on the cleavers that were shrouding the roadside hedge of an arable field boundary near Dudmaston Hall. The bug was 'spotted rather than swept' as Caroline was pursuing an impressive longhorn beetle at the time. The third record came on a lovely, sunny evening at the end of June 2012 when Maria Justamond was visiting Ismore Coppice, south of Shrewsbury. The sighting was made by Maria as she spotted it climbing up some cleavers. Again she only did this whilst trying to approach a long-horned beetle to photograph it. So quite clearly the methodology for spotting the Bordered Shieldbug is to look for long-horned beetles around cleavers when it's sunny and you might see one!

The fourth and most recent record we have had was one found crawling around the shower block at Preston Montford Field Centre (near Shrewsbury) in late July of the same year. It could well have hitched a ride on Ian Cheeseborough (who discovered it) from one of the field sites we had just returned from, or it could have just felt a little grubby, who's to say?

Figure 29. Bordered Shieldbug on foodplant.
Photo: Maria Justamond.

Figure 30. Scale against wrist watch winder (3 mm).
Photo: Maria Justamond.

Figure 31. Close up of border along abdomen.
Photo: Pete Boardman.

Tritomegas bicolor
(Linnaeus, 1758) Pied Shieldbug

GB distribution and status: Southern and central England up to Yorkshire. Uncommon in Wales.

Ease of identification: 1

Ease of finding: 3

Perhaps one of the most spectacularly marked species, this shieldbug is at first surprisingly elusive but with a little practice, or luck, can be found on white dead-nettle and black horehound. Most Shropshire records are associated with white dead-nettle, though Maria Justamond has found adults and nymphs on black horehound in the county. It is seemingly restricted to well-drained soils. The distribution map for Shropshire is quite unlike any other species with a distinct north-eastern bias. I don't imagine this is an accident of field work as the north-western part of the county has been surveyed regularly for shieldbugs by several of us. Indeed when I lived near Oswestry I spent many hours searching road verges and hedge banks where white dead-nettle grew looking for Pied Shieldbug without any success at all. The only successful sighting in the north-west was at Trefonen by Allan Dawes in late April 2011. Looking at the map on the NBN

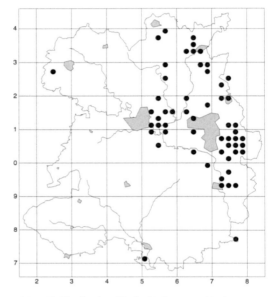

Map 10. Distribution (2km) of *Tritomegas bicolor*.

Gateway (data.nbn.org.uk) suggests the Shropshire distribution fits in well with the national distribution in that the species appears to be restricted to the east of a line that runs roughly from Bristol to Hull. There appear to be very few Welsh records and none from Cheshire to our immediate north. It seems that our county illustrates part of the national east/west boundary of the distribution of this species.

We should perhaps be aware of a lookalike species; Rambur's Pied Shieldbug *Tritomegas sexmaculatus* Rambur, 1839, which has only very recently arrived in the UK and has been found from a couple of sites in Kent. It seems to use the same foodplants as the Pied Shieldbug (with perhaps more emphasis on black horehound than white dead-nettle), but given its current distribution it shouldn't trouble Shropshire shieldbug recorders just yet. [Ed. Keith Fowler encountered Rambur's Pied Shieldbug on a recent trip to Vienna but appears not to have snuck any back and released them as far as anyone can tell].

Figure 32. Photo: Rosemary Winnall.

Figure 33. Late instar nymph. Photo: Jim Shaw.

Figure 34. Pied acrobatics. Photo: Maria Justamond.

Sehirus biguttatus
(Linnaeus, 1758) Cow-wheat Shieldbug

GB distribution and status: Very locally scattered through England and Wales. Scarce.

Ease of identification: 2

Ease of finding: 5

Another Wyre Forest speciality, the first sightings of this uncommon bug were made by Bernard Nau in 1988. He found several of them on a verge at the edge of the Forest in amongst leaf litter where cow-wheat was growing. This information came to us fairly early on in the compilation of historical data in early 2010 and following this lead I visited the Mortimer Forest near Ludlow and spent a few hours on my hands and knees probing in amongst the leaf litter around cow-wheat plants without any success at all. I tried a similar approach at a couple of other sites where cow-wheat is known and again without success. Thankfully the Wyre Forest team were on the ball and spent time sieving litter and achieved success in that way. As John Bingham informed me, one of the locations the shieldbug was found in was wet leaf litter where it was hidden deeply in between the leaf layers. The location was a heather dominated area of woodland on a slope

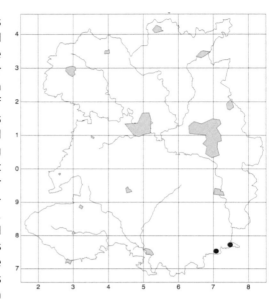

Map 11. Distribution (2km) of *Sehirus biguttatus*.

and it was found after a long and tiring search. The Wyre Forest entomologists are frequently out in many areas of the Forest but have rarely seen the insect which suggests it is probably not something that one might happen across accidentally; rather a lot of effort is needed to find it. The question has been asked whether the insect basks in open ground on warm spring days, as is typical of some of the other closely related shieldbugs? Clearly much more work is needed on establishing where populations are within the Wyre and how best to find them. A distribution map of cow-wheat would show it to be relatively widespread plant across Shropshire and so presumably more colonies of the shieldbug are discretely tucked away. Certainly given the amount of cow-wheat in Mortimer Forest a return trip with a sieve in late summer may well be worth a go.

Figure 35. Cow-wheat Shieldbug. Photo: John Bingham.

Figure 36. Cow-wheat Shieldbug. Photo: John Bingham.

Sehirus luctuosus
Mulsant and Rey, 1886 Forget-me-not Shieldbug

GB distribution and status: Frequent through southern England up to the Humber. Uncommon in Wales.

Ease of identification: 3

Ease of finding: 3

This was another species of shieldbug that was absent from the initial data compilation in late 2009 to early 2010, but it was one of the first species to be added following some sterling and very patient work carried out by Ian Cheeseborough, initially at Grinshill Quarry in late April 2010. Ian picked a sunny, sandy bank with common forget-me-not growing on it and sat himself down and waited, and waited, and waited some more until something moved. Thankfully when something did move it was this species and he started to get his eye in on how and where to find it. No more sightings came that year but the following year several of us found the species from well-drained, south-facing sites with forget-me-not, and this trend continued through 2012 and 2013. We found several of them on a sloped verge outside Llanyblodwell churchyard on a shieldbug field trip in 2012 (and again in 2013), whilst Michelle Furber and Warren

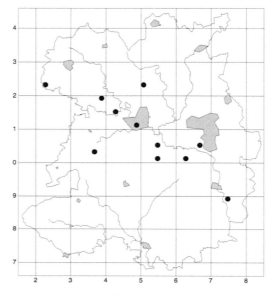

Map 12. Distribution (2km) of *Sehirus luctuosus*.

Putter found the bug on the sands of Venus Bank quarry in 2013 whilst looking for ground beetles. To illustrate that it isn't necessarily habitats of conservation importance that are primarily habitat, the species has been found in gardens at the Greenwood Centre in Ironbridge and Preston Montford Field Centre. Both locations were areas where forget-me-not was growing and both were south-facing parts of the garden with compacted soil.

Figure 37. Forget-me-not Shieldbug.
Photo: Maria Justamond.

Figure 38. Forget-me-not Shieldbug.
Photo: Maria Justamond.

Pentatomidae – the true shieldbugs

The largest group with twenty species in the UK and often called the 'typical shieldbugs'. Twelve of the twenty have been recorded in Shropshire plus a one off occurrence of a rare vagrant. This family has tarsi with three segments (Acanthosomatidae has two segments per tarsi).

Graphosoma lineatum
(Linnaeus, 1758) Striped Shieldbug VAGRANT

GB distribution and status: Rare vagrant.

Ease of identification: 1

Ease of finding: n/a

Little did Ian Thompson know that the plants he had bought from the garden centre had a small hidden population of this stripy bug on them! We may never have got to know about the sudden appearance and disappearance of this vagrant species that is more usually at home in Southern, Central to Northern Europe (www.gbif.com), were it not the garden of an entomologist into which they accidentally arrived! Ian reported seeing quite a number regularly over a several week period during the summer of 1995 when the plants were bought, but the bugs didn't reappear after that. He suggested that several early instars of the nymphs must have been tucked away on the plants when they arrived. A lot of larger garden centres buy in garden plants from nurseries in Holland and so the likelihood is that they'd travelled over on a lorry from the continent, possibly as eggs, and hatched in situ in Ian's Meole Brace garden.

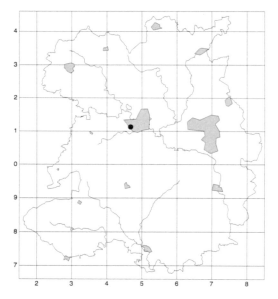

Map 13. Distribution (2km) of *Graphosoma lineatum*.

The arrival and disappearance of this species opens up the wider possibility in this age of globalisation of more unusual species arriving in the county. Pretty much every week there is a newspaper story of some invertebrate purveyor of death arriving on supermarket bananas, or insect carriers... I suspect the prospect of vagrant bugs turning up is something we will have to get used to, though I doubt there will be the same hysteria as witnessed recently in the press by our Shropshire spider enthusiasts.

Figure 39. Striped Shieldbug photographed in France.
Photo: Maria Justamond.

Aelia acuminata
(Linnaeus, 1758) Bishop's Mitre Shieldbug

GB distribution and status: Common in southern and central England up to the Humber, and Wales.

Ease of identification: 1

Ease of finding: 3

The first Shropshire record of this unique looking grassland species was from Cleobury Wood found by John Meiklejohn in 2007 (which again suggests the entry point to Shropshire along the River Severn corridor). Since then it has been found sparingly at sites with well-drained fairly tall grassland including the old mine spoil at Snailbeach (Jones, 2010) and Ifton Meadows, right on the border with Wrexham Borough, suggesting a rapid progress through the county. In 2009 in Shropshire we had a single sighting, 2010 four sightings, 2011 one sighting, 2012 seven sightings and in 2013 we had six sightings of the Bishop's Mitre Shieldbug, so there seems to be a slightly upward trend. The majority seem to have been found by sweeping with a net through tall, dry grassland rather than finding individuals basking on vegetation or crawling over the ground.

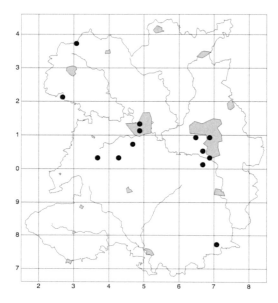

Map 14. Distribution (2km) of *Aelia acuminata*.

There was also an unconfirmed report from the Ludlow area from 2012 but no record was forthcoming. There must be many more potential host sites for this species where long, well drained grassland is found. It is particularly noteworthy that there are so few records in the south of the county which suggests more searching may reveal useful records. Several of us targeted one potential site, the dry meadow at Dudmaston, in 2012 but without luck.

It would be particularly wonderful to find one in a churchyard – think of the press opportunities – the headline writes itself!

Figure 40. Photo: David Williams.

Figure 41. Mating pair, photographed in France.
Photo: Maria Justamond

Figure 42. Bishop's Mitre Shieldbug.
Photo: Maria Justamond.

Neottiglossa pusilla
(Gmelin, 1789) Small Grass Shieldbug

GB distribution and status: Common through southern and central England up to the Humber. Less common in western England. Uncommon in Wales.

Ease of identification: 3

Ease of finding: 3

Though records are relatively few for this small cryptically coloured bug, it is a species that attracts attention as often it is an unexpected find, and therefore people remember when they come across it.

It was found in good numbers in the Wyre Forest during 2013 from grassy woodland rides. Denise and John Bingham found several within a few minutes in Longdon Wood, including some basking on grass stems. Caroline Uff swept one from a recently felled conifer block at Dudmaston woods. The area had started to regenerate with acid grassland species, rosebay willowherb and some bramble.

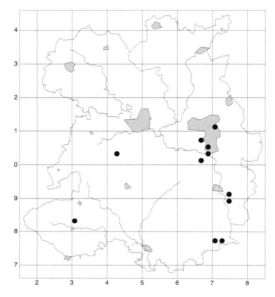

Map 15. Distribution (2km) of *Neottiglossa pusilla*.

Godfrey Blunt recorded one from Forestry Commission site at Bury Ditches on a Shropshire Invertebrates Group visit. It was found beside a wide ride along the southern border of a plantation forest, crawling on open ground in a sunny south-facing spot. The vegetation around was mixed conifer plantation and deciduous oak woodland on heathy acidic soils. He also found one in Malinslee which was seen crawling around on some bare ground amongst dry grassland. Maria Justamond found a nymph of this species at Coalmoor (Telford) in dry grassland where it was sat on a leaf low down in the vegetation. Nigel Cane-Honeysett swept one from sheltered heathland vegetation at the Albion pit mound. Keith Fowler relayed this tale of a hastily convened identification summit on the mound to positively identify the bug.

These sightings suggest micro-climate is pretty important for this bug and warm bare ground in amongst grassland or scrubby habitats may offer good habitat.

Figure 43. Adult from Comer Wood, Dudmaston.
Photo: David Williams

Figure 44. Final instar nymph. Photo: Maria Justamond.

Figure 45. Adult from Pulverbatch. Photo: David Williams.

Eysarcoris venustissimus
(Schrank, 1776) Woundwort Shieldbug

GB distribution and status: Common in southern and central England up to the Humber, but less common in Wales.

Ease of identification: 2

Ease of finding: 2

I have a soft spot for this species of shieldbug. Perhaps it is the slightly smaller or the rounded shape but I've always considered it a personal favourite. Perhaps it was one of the first slightly less common species I noticed? When we put together the original maps in early 2010 however it was a species with only half a dozen dots on the map but recorder effort has started to show the true extent of its distribution in the county.

As the name suggests the shieldbug is associated with hedge woundwort but all of the early sightings I made of this species were on white dead-nettle. Several recorders including Jacki and Clive Dyer, Anne and Jim Shaw, Nigel Jones, and I have this species in our gardens. In mine, hedge woundwort grows as an encouraged weed in a shrub bed and revels in late afternoon sun. These conditions seem to suit the bugs and they can often be seen basking. Indeed the majority of sightings are from hedge woundwort but nettle, bramble and the aforementioned white dead-nettle are also mentioned in recorders' sightings.

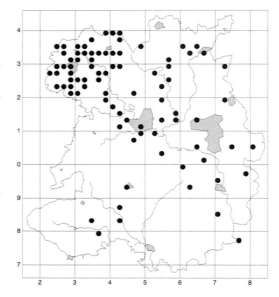

Map 16. Distribution (2km) of *Eysarcoris venustissimus*.

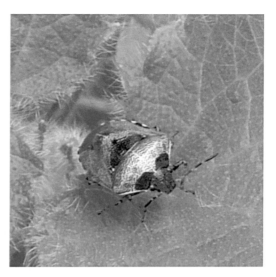

Figure 47. Woundwort Shieldbug. Photo: Jim Cresswell.

Figure 46. Woundwort Shieldbug. Photo: David Williams.

Figure 48. Woundwort Shieldbug. Photo: Clive Dyer.

Palomena prasina
(Linnaeus, 1761) Green Shieldbug

GB distribution and status: Common in England up to Yorkshire, and common in Wales. Rare in Scotland.

Ease of identification: 1

Ease of finding: 1

I helped out on a BBC Summer of Wildlife event recently at Sutton Park near Birmingham where I had a pinned insect display and literature, including the FSC fold-out chart to Shieldbugs, on show. Many hundreds of families trooped through during the day and looked at the insects and books, and virtually everyone commented that they recognised 'that green bug' which we would know as *Palomena prasina*, the Green Shieldbug. Some keen gardeners had a bit of a moan at the damage they are alleged to do to some fruit and vegetables in their plots or allotments but the reaction was in no way as hysterical as it was to a specimen of the Vine Weevil nearby. Thankfully it appears there is no targeted mass elimination aimed at the Green Shieldbug and the Royal Horticultural Society deems them harmless on their website (apps.rhs.org.uk). The species is however treated more as a true pest species elsewhere in Europe as they can cause significant damage to hazelnut kernels in orchards in southern Europe and Turkey (Saruhan *et al.*, 2010).

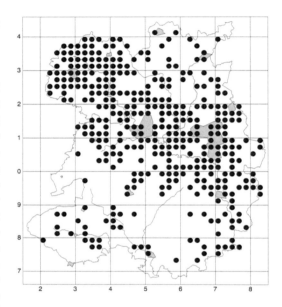

Map 17. Distribution (2km) of *Palomena prasina*.

In Shropshire this is a ubiquitous creature and not unsurprisingly has topped the most frequently recorded bug table with 352 tetrads housing the creature. This would definitely be one of the 'par' species and be expected to be found somewhere in every tetrad. Whilst it is very easy to identify it from egg to adult, it should be noted that a lookalike is heading our way in the shape of the Southern Green Shieldbug (see page 72). The differences are enough to fairly easily separate the two species as adults but the nymphal stages are very different indeed. This species is being treated a little circumspectly by the RHS who suggest it may be in need of control should numbers spiral.

Most recorders report sightings of this Green Shieldbug from rough vegetation such as nettles and brambles etc and low hedgerows from 0.5 m to 1.5 m above ground level, though occasional records have been noted from trees including hawthorn, wych elm, oak, sweet chestnut and hazel.

Figure 49. Photo: Clive Dyer.

Figure 50. Mating adults and onlookers. Photo: Nigel Jones.

Figure 51. Final instar nymph. Photo: Jim Shaw.

Dolycoris baccarum
(Linnaeus, 1758) Sloe Shieldbug

GB distribution and status: Common through southern and central England up to Cumbria. Common in Wales. Less frequent in northern England and southern Scotland.

Ease of identification: 1

Ease of finding: 1

The Sloe Shieldbug is also known as the Hairy Shieldbug. However the alternative name can be misleading, as by the time the bug reaches adulthood its hairs can be overlooked without close inspection, although the hairs that cloak the nymphal stages are very obvious indeed. The name 'Sloe Bug' often causes confusion itself as this leads to the assumption of an association with blackthorn. It seems however that the bug is named after the purple colour of a squashed sloe berry.

This is a very familiar species in Shropshire and elsewhere, and is one of the first along with Green Shieldbug that the shieldbug-watcher gets to know. It can be found in most vegetated habitats having emerged from hibernation. Later in the summer is often associated with creeping thistle or other thistle species (we have one record of an association with woolly thistle). My dog

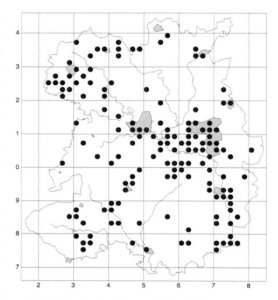

Map 18. Distribution (2km) of *Dolycoris baccarum*.

walking activities again gave me the opportunity to count up to a dozen individuals on a patch of creeping thistle over a two-week period in August 2011. Numbers differed slightly each day but there was a presence throughout. Hawkins (2003) notes that the bugs leave the thistles before the seed heads open and go into hibernation in late September. Nobody seems to have speculated why thistles are chosen but presumably the prickly appearance of the thistles might dissuade predation? This would certainly make sense and also why the bugs leave before the birds arrive to feed on the thistle seeds in late summer.

In warm open habitats observations have been made of large numbers wandering around the ground on the open limestone at Lea Quarry, and Bull Farm, both on along Wenlock Edge. When Maria Justamond discovered Small Grass Shieldbug at Coalmoor she struggled to get close to the insect to photograph it due to the numbers of adults and nymphs of Sloe Bug wandering within the immediate area.

Figure 52. Sloe Shieldbug. Photo: David Williams.

Figure 53. Hairy nymph. Photo: Maria Justamond.

Figure 54. Sloe Shieldbug. Photo: Sue Swindells.

Piezodorus lituratus
(Fabricius, 1789) Gorse Shieldbug

GB distribution and status: Fairly common through England, Wales and Scotland.

Ease of identification: 2

Ease of finding: 3

Our original map of distribution for this species in early 2010 comprised of only a handful of sites but this has been improved dramatically by recorders targeting areas of gorse throughout the county. Records have also been boosted as this is a species where the eggs are easily spotted with a bit of practice as they are often laid on the flower calyx or pod. Western gorse and common gorse seem to be equally well used in the county, though David Williams found several bugs using western gorse only on a site that was predominantly common gorse. Although the vast majority of records are from either western or common gorse, there are a few other sightings from other plants including broom and quince (Sue Swindells), birch (Shropshire Invertebrates Group), hawthorn (Allan Dawes), and bramble (Sue Hiatt).

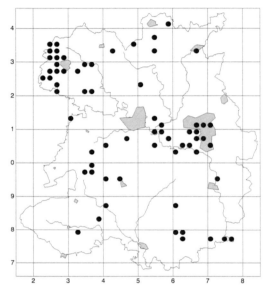

Map 19. Distribution (2km) of *Piezodorus lituratus*.

Godfrey Blunt commented that our map for this species is very similar to the distribution of micro-lepidoptera that feed on gorse which suggests either we've covered the same ground for both groups of animals, or that the maps suggest the main focus of distribution for these species is now known.

Figure 55. Gorse Shieldbug – summer colour form.
Photo: Sue Swindells.

Figure 56. Gorse Shieldbug – spring colour form.
Photo: David Williams.

Figure 57. Gorse Shieldbug eggs. Photo: Pete Boardman.

Pentatoma rufipes
(Linnaeus, 1758) Forest Bug

GB distribution and status: Common through England, Wales and Scotland.
Ease of identification: 2
Ease of finding: 2

Although this shieldbug is sometimes referred to as the 'Red-legged Shieldbug', this alternative name can lead to confusion because the bug can have black legs. The similar Spiked Shieldbug has bright shining orange-red legs, which again can lead to confusion in identification for beginners at first glance.

This is a predatory shieldbug that is found in well-vegetated places so could and does turn up anywhere. It is a regular at moth light as reported by Anne and Jim Shaw, and Graham Wenman. During 2013 alone it was reported from ash, oak, bramble, sycamore, sallow, wych elm, field maple, Himalayan balsam, gorse, a fence post, and a car windscreen.

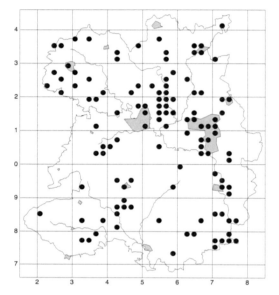

Map 20. Distribution (2km) of *Pentatoma rufipes*.

Whilst not a Shropshire anecdote, in 2011 my wife and I were travelling upon the London Underground when I became aware of a commotion further down the carriage. People were avoiding a particular seat, and some were pointing, one lady screamed. Thankfully the carriage was not particularly rammed full of people so I made my way along to see what the cause was of discomfort. A solitary Forest Bug was sat on the seat back, presumably having snook onto the train on someone's rucksack or coat. I encouraged it onto my hand whilst I reassured the other passengers with the phrase 'It's ok, I'm an entomologist!'

A fellow passenger produced a very nearly empty matchbox from his pocket, emptied the few remaining matches and proffered the box to me as a carriage for the Forest Bug. I persuaded the bug in, and people went back to their own insular lives whilst the train proceeded to the next stop. I introduced the liberated bug to a handy leaf on a tree in Soho Square before we all carried on with our evening.

Figure 58. Note dark legs on this individual. Photo: Pete Boardman.

Figure 59. Forest Shieldbug. Photo: David Williams.

Figure 60. Final instar. Photo: Pete Boardman.

Eurydema oleracea
(Linnaeus, 1758) Brassica Bug

GB distribution and status: Common in southern England then scarce up to the southern Midlands.

Ease of identification: 2

Ease of finding: 5

This species of shieldbug is a bit of an enigma with only one sighting in Shropshire to date made by Denise and John Bingham in the Wyre Forest on 22 May 2007. The bug was encountered in a sunny glade in Nailing Coppice. The bug is most usually associated with horse-radish but a number of other crucifers are known to be used. Kevin McGee found the bug in Worcestershire in 2007 on oil-seed rape flowers in two locations (Meiklejohn, 2011) but it seemingly remains rare in that county. The association of the bug with oil-seed rape must offer up an interesting opportunity given the massive level of cropping seen across the landscape of agricultural Shropshire, though I suspect few entomologists would be that interested in spending time searching for the inevitable needle in the haystack. It may therefore be more preferable to target any known stands of horse-radish instead.

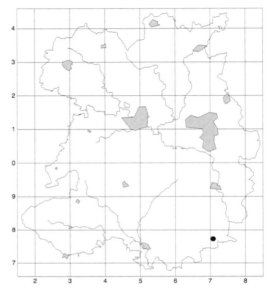

Map 21. Distribution (2km) of *Eurydema oleracea*.

Figure 62. Pale form Brassica Bug in Brittany.
Photo: Maria Justamond.

Figure 61. Red form Brassica Bug. Photo: John Bingham.

Figure 63. Red form Brassica Bug. Photo: John Bingham.

Picromerus bidens
(Linnaeus, 1758) Spiked Shieldbug

GB distribution and status: Common through England, Wales and Scotland.

Ease of identification: 2

Ease of finding: 2

It is with a sense of shock I have just discovered the dear old Spiked Shieldbug has now been called the 'Spined Shieldbug' on the NBN Gateway! Spined, sadly is not a typographical error but another ghastly Americanism that has crept into our language. I feel a campaign coming on and protests on the streets! Do these people always have to meddle with good old fashioned vernacular names? Anyhow, pending e-petition aside, this is a widespread predatory bug of sheltered edge habitats. I personally always tend to find it on sheltered, sunny areas of bramble but there could be some bias in my observations. Sue Swindells also found the majority of her 2013 sightings on bramble in sunny situations so there may be something in it.

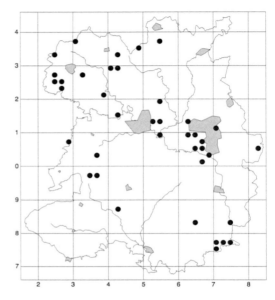

Map 22. Distribution (2km) of *Picromerus bidens.*

I witnessed an assembly of early instars scatter from the grouping on top of a bramble leaf to all hide beneath and on accompanying leaves when I prodded my finger their way whilst visiting Llanymynech Rocks recently. The instars started to reassemble as a group some few minutes later when convinced the danger had gone. Presumably this scatter routine is designed to confuse predators or confuse observers like me.

Figure 64. Spiked Shieldbug with prey. Photo: Sue Swindells.

Figure 65. Early nymphs Spiked Shieldbug. Photo: Maria Justamond.

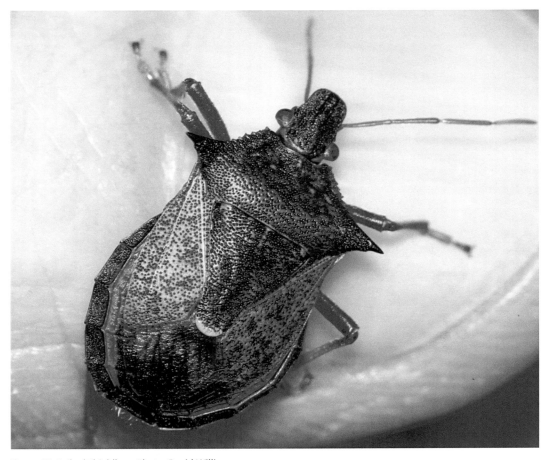

Figure 66. Spiked Shieldbug. Photo: David Williams.

Troilus luridus
(Fabricius, 1775) Bronze Shieldbug

GB distribution and status: Common through England and Wales. Uncommon in Scotland.

Ease of identification: 3

Ease of finding: 2

Perhaps one of the more obvious species to identify as a nymph, the adults are however easily confused with a few other species until familiarisation is gained. This is another shieldbug that predates other insects such as larvae or small adult beetles, but will also feed upon plant material. The colouring through the nymphal stages gets more garish and shinier as they approach adulthood with a clear green sheen in the final instar and fresh adults. Due to their food preferences they can turn up in vegetation just about anywhere and records are widespread in Shropshire.

During 2012 I observed a final instar nymph on a hawthorn hedgerow along my regular dog-walking and shieldbug observing route. It stayed roughly in the same place for three or four days (based on when I was passing each day). On the following day I spotted it had emerged as an

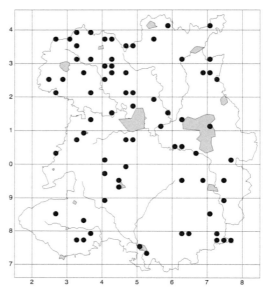

Map 23. Distribution (2km) of *Troilus luridus*.

adult and was in teneral colouration of orange and pink, though the tell tale yellow bands on the antennae were still obvious. I moved it pretty much straight away as a tractor and flail were heading up the hedge line to massacre the hedge, quite typically removing all hope of a berry crop for the winter birds and a safe haven for many other creatures.

Figure 67. Bronze Shieldbug. Photo: David Williams.

Figure 68. Final instar Bronze Shieldbug.
Photo: David Williams.

Figure 69. Final instar Bronze Shieldbug.
Photo: Maria Justamond.

Rhacognathus punctatus
(Linnaeus, 1758) Heather Shieldbug

GB distribution and status: Infrequent through England, Wales and Scotland.

Ease of identification: 2

Ease of finding: 4

If ever there was a species of shieldbug that attained legendary status for some recorders in the county it is this one and there are some who have paid a very high price indeed for its pursuit! The first record came to light as part of the compilation of records carried out by Liverpool Museum as part of their survey report in the early 1990's of entomological work done at Fenn's, Whixall and Bettisfield Mosses NNR. This was followed in 2002 by a specimen collected in sweep net samples on The Stiperstones NNR by Ian Cheeseborough and identified by the late Peter Skidmore. Peter commented in the survey report to the then site manager, Tom Wall, on the unusual location saying he was more familiar with the species as one of wet heath rather than drier upland habitats. (Skidmore would have presumably been familiar with the bug from the Thorne Moors NNR complex in Yorkshire).

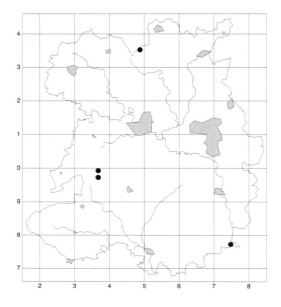

Map 24. Distribution (2km) of *Rhacognathus punctatus.*

Nearly a decade passed without further sightings until Brett Westwood found the bug on a Wyre Forest Study Group outing at Withybed Wood in 2010 and that encouraged searches elsewhere now that we knew it was still active in the county. Maria Justamond visited Fenn's, Whixall and Bettisfield Mosses NNR to search for it on an historical site but unfortunately ended the day being airlifted to hospital by air ambulance with a badly dislocated ankle for her troubles.

A group of dipterists including myself did however catch up with it on Whixall Moss in June 2012 whilst looking for the hairy canary fly *Phaonia jaroschewskii* (Schnabl, 1888) with Steven Falk (Buglife). Gordon Leel found the shieldbug, whilst we were all sheltering from a particularly heavy rainstorm amongst the alders and birches that fringe the uncut area of the bog (known locally as the Cranberry Beds). Whilst we were ecstatic at finding the bug we were nevertheless all tinged with guilt that Maria was not amongst our number that day, for more than anyone she deserved to see it. [Ed. Keith Fowler pointed out that I had omitted to mention the kiss I firmly planted on Gordon's cheek on his rediscovery of the bug. Corrected Keith!]

Further to the re-finding on Whixall Moss, a couple of months later Stuart Edmunds found the insect again on the Stiperstones NNR showing that there are at least three potentially stable populations in Shropshire represented on lowland raised mire (Whixall), upland moorland (Stiperstones) and lowland heath in ancient woodland (Wyre Forest). However despite these populations existing they appear to be reasonably localised and difficult to find. The one obvious place where the creature should be located and hasn't to date is the expanse of upland heather (wet in places) that is the Long Mynd. Some searches were carried out during 2013 however this year was not a good shieldbug year due to poor weather.

The other potential factor in regards population size at any one particular site may be affected by the rise and fall in the population of its main food source, larvae of the heather beetle *Lochmaea suturalis* (Thomson, 1866). These have thrived in recent years due to wet summers and mild winters and so therefore the more recent sightings may have been in response to a surge in heather beetle activity?

Figure 70. Heather Shieldbug. Photo: Pete Boardman.

Zicrona caerulea
(Linnaeus, 1758) Blue Bug

GB distribution and status: Common through England and Wales. Uncommon in Scotland.
Ease of identification: 1
Ease of finding: 3

This is another of the predatory species of shieldbug and they are known to feed on flea beetles (Coleoptera: Chrysomelidae). I was first introduced to the species by Ian Cheeseborough who had found them on a number of occasions in Lilleshall Quarry (Wenlock Edge) where they were to be found in a very specific type of habitat. In the quarry bottom slightly sunken areas had become sodden and had been colonised by marsh willowherb where the shieldbugs were to be found low down in the vegetation presumably searching for chrysomelid beetles associated with the willowherb. Godfrey Blunt reported the bug from Chelmarsh in amongst *Phragmites* reed swamp where tall fen vegetation was dominated by great willowherb. On both occasions the shieldbugs were found on warm spring days in reasonable numbers. At Crosemere and Sweatmere members of the Shropshire Invertebrates Group found the bug in good numbers from tall herbaceous vegetation, again on damp soils, with one in the bole of a tree in the vicinity.

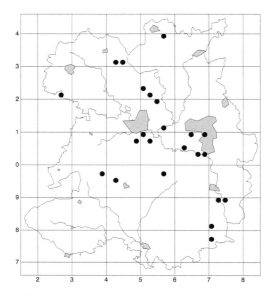

Map 25. Distribution (2km) of *Zicrona caerulea*.

Other records include those that come from the edge of the Bomere Pool, the damper areas of Shawbury Heath (where a number were recorded quite frequently throughout 2013), and from the Ercall Quarry by Amanda Brown and Glen Forde. Given the availability of damp habitats within the Meres and Mosses Natural Area of North Shropshire it should be far more widespread than the current map suggests.

Whilst mostly found in wet to damp habitats there are instances of this species being found in far drier habitats than might otherwise be initially expected, such as at dry limestone of Llanymynech Rocks, and the ash tip at Devil's Dingle at Buildwas but chalk downland is used in the south of England so perhaps we should not be too guided by our association of this bug to damp habitats.

Figure 71. Blue Bug. Photo: Maria Justamond.

Figure 72. Blue Bug. Photo: Maria Justamond.

Coreoidea – leatherbugs, scentless plant bugs, spurge bugs

Coreidae – the leatherbugs

The leatherbugs, or as the Americans call them, squash-bugs are often called 'honorary shieldbugs' as they resemble them in at least size and are generally recorded by people looking for shieldbugs.

Leatherbugs have antennae comprised of four segments with the basal segment often swollen, whereas the shieldbugs have antennae with five segments.

Coreus marginatus
(Linnaeus, 1758) Dock Bug

GB distribution and status: Very common the south and central England up to the Midlands. Frequent along the Welsh coast.

Ease of identification: 1

Ease of finding: 2

This leatherbug is fairly frequently encountered though it can be surprisingly absent at times and searches in north and west of the county have proved largely fruitless, even in perfect habitat of sheltered dock plants. It is perhaps that we are at the edge of its national distribution, or perhaps the sandy soils of the south-west and central areas suit it better? Currently all large brown leatherbugs that we see are this species though we need to take note of the northward march of the Box Bug (see page 73) which has a narrower connexivum than the Dock Bug.

Where noted the dock species on which the bug has been found is broad dock, however we have few actual notes of the precise dock species. Dock Bugs are also seen relatively frequently away from dock and 2013 records include sightings on nettle, ivy, hogweed, and bramble.

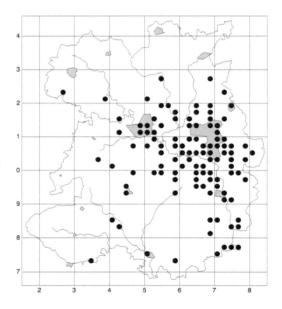

Map 26. Distribution (2km) of *Coreus marginatus*.

Figure 73. Dock Bug. Photo: Jim Cresswell.

Figure 74. Congregation of Dock Bugs. Photo: David Williams.

Coriomeris denticulatus
(Scopoli, 1763) Denticulate Leatherbug

GB distribution and status: Common in southern and central England in a rough line from Bristol to Hull. A few coastal records from northern England. Frequent along the southern Welsh coast and a few records on the northern Welsh coast.

Ease of identification: 3

Ease of finding: 4

The word 'denticulate' refers to the finely toothed, or notched pronotum that is coated in stiff bristles on its surface and around its edge. Steve Judd of Liverpool Museum initially found this leatherbug at Llanymynech Heritage Area as part of the entomological survey the Museum carried out there for Shropshire Council in 1996 (Judd, 1996). The bug is most notably recorded from legumes, such as black medick and clover, and is found most frequently on sandy or limestone soils. Although the Heritage Area is not particularly free-draining or calcareous it is a neighbour of the Llanymynech Rocks SWT reserve which very much is and comprises limestone grassland and old quarry.

Llanymynech remained the only known site until 2012 when Denticulate Leatherbug was found in grassland close to and on the dry ash beds at Buildwas, plus the open limestone quarry habitat

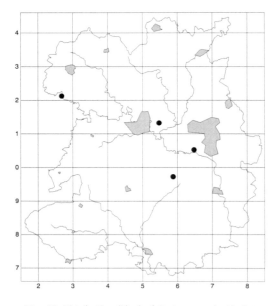

Map 27. Distribution (2km) of *Coriomerus denticulatus*.

of Wenlock Edge. More surprisingly, it was found on the office window of the building in which Maria Justamond works at Upton Magna. Has the insect suddenly become more widespread in Shropshire in the last few years or are we again finding it now we know what we are looking for, and now that more people are aware of it and are looking?

Figure 75. Denticulate at Buildwas. Photo: Nigel Jones.

Figure 76. Denticulate leatherbug on window. Photo: Maria Justamond.

Figure 77. Denticulate underside on window. Photo: Maria Justamond.

Leptoglossus occidentalis
(Heidemann, 1910) Western Conifer Seedbug VAGRANT

GB distribution and status: Throughout England. Frequent in Wales and rare in Scotland.

Ease of identification: 1

Ease of finding: n/a

We were ready for this beast as there had been quite a lot of publicity ahead of its arrival in Shropshire with naturalists and particularly moth trappers asked to keep a look out for it. The Food and Environmental Research Agency (FERA) and Forest Research put out a PDF document showing what the bug looked like and detailed its arrival in the UK where it was first spotted in Weymouth in 2009. This American invader of Europe rapidly spread following that first spotting and the worry was that as a pest of conifer trees (particularly Douglas fir) it could cause havoc in the UK's plantations. This appears not to have happened (yet!), which some may view as a pity.

The first sighting of the bug was made by Dan Wrench after one alighted on his office window at the Shirehall in Shrewsbury. It seemed a particularly dignified way of making the Shropshire list, first stopping by to see Shropshire

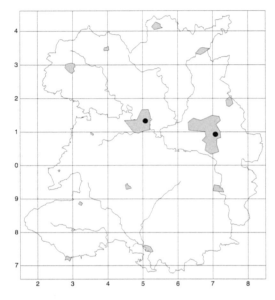

Map 28. Distribution (2km) of *Leptoglossus occidentalis*.

Council's biodiversity officer! It certainly ensured that news of its arrival spread quickly. The suspected mass influx then failed to arrive and no reports were received by moth trappers in Shropshire until Graham Statham reported that he had seen 'an odd bug' at his moth trap in 2012 which he had photographed but hadn't got around to identifying. This emerged at a shieldbug training day and so was a particularly pleasing outcome of the day.

The species is very readily identified by the orangey-brown colouration and the swollen hind tibiae that instantly single it out as something very different. Were it to be widespread I am sure that we would have been receiving plenty of photos in this age of camera phones and online biodiversity.

Figure 78. Specimen from Jim Shaw. Photo: Pete Boardman.

Rhopalidae – the scentless plant bugs or glass-winged bugs

There are eleven species of Rhopalid bug in the UK and four of them have been found in Shropshire. Hawkins (2003) states the position of the stink gland as a separating factor from similar families. Barnard (2011) considers them a little-known family amongst the hemiptera, whilst the name glass-winged bugs are offered as an alternative name by the Southampton Natural History Society (2007) in their atlas.

Corizus hyoscyami
(Linnaeus, 1758)

GB distribution and status: Common in southern England and Wales.

Ease of identification: 2

Ease of finding: 2

At one time seeing this red and black bug in Shropshire was something of a special occasion and something noteworthy. At that time the bug was seemingly pretty much confined to old sand quarries or dry grassland or woodland in the south of the county but in recent years numbers appear to have increased and it is a regular find these days around Shropshire. Keith Fowler found the bug at Colemere Country Park on a shieldbug field meeting in September 2011 which showed how far north the bug had reached and following that it has turned up in several other locations around north Shropshire. The distribution maps clearly suggest the passage of the bug up the River Severn corridor (oh yes that again!).

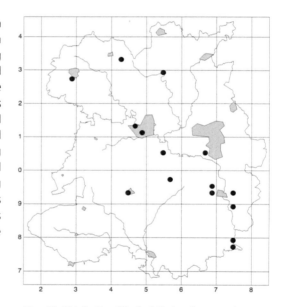

Map 29. Distribution (2km) of *Corizus hyoscyami*.

Figure 79. *Corizus hyoscyami*. Photo: Nigel Jones.

Figure 80. *Corizus hyoscyami*. Photo: Sue Swindells.

Rhopalus subrufus
(Gmelin, 1788)

GB distribution and status: Common in southern and central England. Less frequent north and west of the Midlands except Yorkshire where it is reasonably common. Frequent in Wales.

Ease of identification: 3

Ease of finding: 3

There are four species of this genus in the UK and currently only one is found in Shropshire, *Rhopalus subrufus*. Two of the species are rare and restricted to the south of England, but *R. parumpunctatus* Schilling, 1829 is one to keep our eyes out for as its national distribution map shows a presence in the English midlands and also records from Wales. *R. subrufus* has two features to easily separate it; the connexivum is white and black striped, and the scutellum ends in a white dot and is bifid (two-pronged). *R parumpunctatus* has a red and black connexivum and the scutellum is not white-tipped and ends in a single point. It might be wise therefore to double check these features for all subsequent finds of this species to ensure a correct identification is being made and that a new species is not being overlooked.

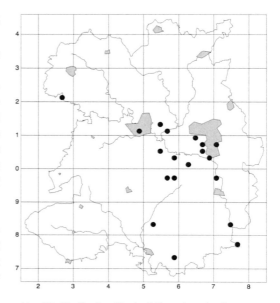

Map 30. Distribution (2km) of *Rhopalus subrufus*.

The map nicely illustrates the River Severn corridor effect with the majority of records in that route. Virtually all Shropshire records are from dry sites be they grassland, woodland or old quarry sites. Shropshire records range from mid-April through until early September.

One particular record came from Sue and Gwyn Hiatt who visited a now notorious site near Telford to look for shieldbugs one late afternoon in June 2012. Sue and Gwyn put the unusually populated location down (which she described as 'perfect shieldbug habitat') to people out enjoying the fresh air on a summer's day. Sue and Gwyn spent time sweeping the vegetation, and then searching for bugs on all fours (as did some of the other attendees there it transpires but they were searching (and by the sound of it finding) something else entirely! Sue wonders what was made of the cameras and notebooks her and husband Gwyn were carrying?

Figure 81. *Rhopalus subrufus*. Photo: David Williams.

Figure 82. *Rhopalus subrufus* nymph. Photo: Maria Justamond

Figure 83. *Rhopalus subrufus*. Photo: Maria Justamond.

Myrmus miriformis
(Fallén, 1807)

GB distribution and status: Relatively common throughout England and Wales.

Ease of identification: 3

Ease of finding: 3

I suspect one of the reasons why this species is seemingly restricted in its distribution in Shropshire is that is often mistaken for a mirid bug (Miridae) and so ignored by those wishing not to get involved in the identification of quite a difficult group of insects. A quick glance at the head of the bug though would forestall any confusion as it has ocelli or rudimentary eyes which the Miridae lack. Further confusion follows unfortunately as males have two colour forms, a green one and a brown one. Females are always green. David Williams' photograph of a pair mating shows a brown male mating with a green female to illustrate the difference.

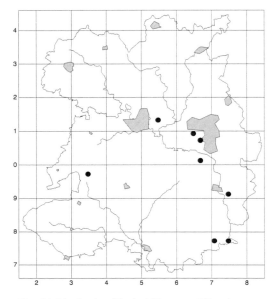

Map 31. Distribution (2km) of *Myrmus miriformis.*

Hawkins (2003) states that this is a species of dry grassland with the majority of sites in Surrey being on acidic soils. In Shropshire there is no one real common thread to the habitats where this bug has been recorded yet. It was first noted in 1985 (an untypically old record by the standards of our database) from Haughmond Hill, a mixture of forestry with some heathy grassland, then in 1999 Liverpool Museum's survey team found it at the Ercall SWT reserve. The Ercall is an old quarry with an aspect of ancient semi-natural woodland, scrub, grassland, and bare ground. Records were then made in more recent times from the Wyre Forest, a couple of grasslands at Ironbridge (dry and damp), the Bog Mine site at Pennerley (damp grassland), and the grassland by Comber Wood at Dudmaston (dry and heathy). Records range from mid-July to the end of September.

Figure 81. *Myrmus miriformis* green form. Photo: John Bingham.

Figure 82. *Myrmus miriformis* mating pair. Photo: David Williams.

Stictopleurus abutilon
(Rossi, 1790)

GB distribution and status: Common around the Thames Gateway. Widespread but uncommon through southern and central England.

Ease of identification: 5

Ease of finding: 3

This bug is one that is known to be heading north from its traditional Thames Gateway distribution. The current map displayed on the NBN Gateway would make our record the most northerly UK one recorded (though the distribution maps may not be totally up to date). The bug was swept from a dry sandy area, with much exposed sand, at Eardington Quarry in July 2006 by Nigel Jones. Identification was made by Nigel and checked by Bernard Nau. The identification is based upon the round black marks on the top corners of the pronotum. The similar *Stictopleurus punctatonervosus* (Goeze, 1778) has semi-circular marks on the pronotum, rather than fully circular marks. As well as dry grassland, as stated on British Bugs (www.british-bugs.org.uk), most dry habitats could well be suitable for the bug. Hawkins (2003) lists heathland, chalk grassland, and a clay pit as the sites where the bug was found in Surrey. He also mentioned adults and nymphs were swept off rough hawkbit which may offer an ecological lead.

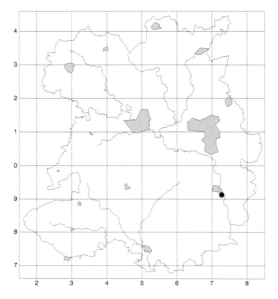

Map 32. Distribution (2km) of *Stictopleurus abutilon*.

The Bridgnorth area is heavily represented by old and current sand quarries and dry grassland on sand, and is severely underworked in terms of its bug fauna. Certainly more targeting of these sites is bound to produce more interesting finds in the future, possibly including this species.

Figure 83. *Stictopleurus abutilon* via Nigel Jones.
Photo: Pete Boardman.

Figure 84. Pronotum detail of *Stictopleurus abutilon*.
Photo: Pete Boardman.

Stenocephalidae – the spurge bugs

There are two species of spurge bug in the UK of the same genera however one is found in our region. The other spurge bug is associated with coastal species of spurge so should not worry us in terms of confusion.

Dicranocephalus medius
(Mulsant and Rey, 1870) 'a spurge bug'

GB distribution and status: Uncommon in southern and central England.

Ease of identification: 3

Ease of finding: 4

This spurge bug (there are two UK species) is associated with wood spurge and is quite a difficult species to find as it is said to spend most of its time hidden at the base of spurge plants (Hawkins 2003). They do however occasionally climb up onto flowers where Kevin McGee photographed one in the Wyre Forest on 26 May 2007 (Wyre Forest Study Group Review, 2007). The Wyre Forest remains its only known location in Shropshire where records range in date from 4 May until 18 June with a peak in late May. Perhaps like the Cow-wheat Shieldbug this surely another one that should be recorded elsewhere in the county with some targeted fieldwork. Again Mortimer Forest near Ludlow would be an obvious place to start as wood spurge is relatively common there. A sunny day in late May would perhaps be a good time to start looking.

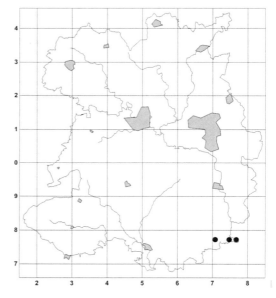

Map 32. Distribution (2km) of *Dicranocephalus medius*.

Figure 85. *Dicranocephalus medius*. Photo: John Bingham.

Figure 86. *Dicranocephalus medius*. Photo: John Bingham.

Shieldbugs and allies that we haven't yet recorded or those that might be coming our way

Whilst we have had several pairs of eyes looking out for which species are at large in Shropshire there is of course the likelihood that we have missed species already here, or might expect to find others arriving shortly. We are particularly lucky to have some very 'nosy neighbours' to our south who are keeping us abreast of the situation in Worcestershire, either directly or through publication in the Wyre Forest Review or the Worcestershire Record. Whilst there may be more species that could be mentioned here, the ones I have noted are the ones mentioned in those publications, or by looking at the current distribution maps on the NBN Gateway and seeing species that might arrive in our county.

Pentatomidae

Eurydema ornata (Linnaeus, 1758) Ornate Shieldbug. Though a recent colonist of southern England one of these colourful shieldbugs turned up in a delivery of broccoli in Worcestershire in 2000 (Meiklejohn, 2011). The bug is associated with crucifers including cabbages, radish, etc. Given the current boom in organic vegetable boxes there is scope for the further spread of this species into our region.

Nezara viridula (Linnaeus, 1758) Southern Green Shieldbug. The nearest record I am aware of to Shropshire is from Birmingham (on the NBN Gateway map) but it might not be too unrealistic to expect this species to turn up at some point in Telford or Shrewsbury as it seems to move with people. It is a species resident in Africa and southern Europe originally, but one that has spread along with human trade and migration.

Thyreocoridae

This bug belongs to the Thyreocoridae, a family we have not yet encountered in this atlas so far. It was treated by some as a sub-family of the Cydnidae, but lacks the tibial spines of that family.

Thyreocoris scarabaeoides (Linnaeus, 1758) Scarab Shieldbug (called Negro Bug or Ebony Bug in some publications). This is a small (approx 4 mm) metallic black shieldbug similar to members of the Cydnidae and is associated with violets growing on dry sandy or chalky soils and is said to be found in leaf litter and moss in these habitats (Hawkins 2003). The map on the NBN Gateway suggests we may well have this species lurking somewhere in the county with Llanymynech Rocks, Jones' Rough, Wenlock Edge, Dudmaston and the wider Bridgnorth area all prospective candidates for its discovery. Adults are photographed on the British Bugs website in April, May and August but potentially could be seen in other months too.

Coreidae

Arenocoris fallenii (Schilling, 1829) Fallen's Leatherbug. In a recent communication Brett Westwood suggested we should keep our eyes open for this species which he recently found under common stork's-bill on dredged river sand near Worcester. I spent part of a day with John Handley in 2012 looking for it around common stork's-bill around the Bridgnorth area without success but it may turn up.

Ceraleptus lividus Stein, 1858 Slender-horned Leatherbug. This species was found by Jane and Dave Scott at their smallholding near Stourport-upon-Severn, some 10-15 miles south of the Shropshire border. Their first record was an adult on the 19ᵗʰ April 2011, but most adults and late instar nymphs have been found in the August to October periods since then. They are found in the well-drained sandy grasslands there and Jane notes that the bugs prefer to hide below short vegetation or very near ground level. Therefore the 'hands and knees approach' seems to work best in finding them. They also note that *Coriomeris denticulatus* occupies similar habitat on the same site. Perhaps it would not be too unrealistic to assume that this species could well have moved north recently into similarly warm, sheltered, species-rich acid grassland on sands adjacent to the River Severn in Shropshire.

Gonocerus acuteangulatus (Goeze, 1778) Box Bug. A third species of leatherbug to look out for this species was formerly restricted to Box Hill in Surrey but has recently been expanding northwards. The nearest I am aware of was the one noted by Andrew Curran in Worcestershire Record (April, 2011) at Edgbaston near Birmingham.

Alydidae

Another family not represented yet in this atlas, the Alydidae or the broad-headed bugs are represented by this single species in the UK.

Alydus calcaratus (Linnaeus, 1758) Again the NBN Gateway map suggests we might like keep an eye out for this large black bug found on dry heathland. Sadly lowland heathland is not a very common habitat in Shropshire though it does exist at Prees Heath, and in remnants elsewhere such as The Cliffe.

Rhopalidae

Chorosoma schillingi (Schilling,1829). This is another species that the national maps suggest we should be recording in Shropshire. It may well have been overlooked due to its similarity to several species of mirid bugs and because it is fantastically well camouflaged against grasses.

Rhopalus parumpunctatus Schilling, 1829. See account for *R. subrufus* on page 64.

Stictopleurus punctatonervosus (Goeze, 1778) The NBN Gateway map of distribution suggest this species should perhaps have been the first one of the *Stictopleurus* species to have arrived in Shropshire but we currently have no records. Rather, the more scarcely distributed *S. abutilon* is known from one site in the county. *S. punctatonervosus* is another species that has been intercepted by Jane and Dave Scott in Stourport-upon-Severn which suggests once more the River Severn corridor is the main conduit north for potential Shropshire shieldbugs and allies. This was another species first noted by Jane and Dave in 2011, and by 2012 large numbers had been noted with more than thirty individuals recorded and mating observed. Numbers however appear to have dipped dramatically in 2013 (presumably due to the cold spring), and only a couple were recorded in their garden later in the year. Jane notes that the bugs seem to spend a lot of time around the flower heads of lavender and marjoram. Jane also notes that she has encountered one of the bugs outside her garden about half a mile north close once more to the River Severn. This suggests the potential for further discoveries in our county in suitable habitat.

A final note – one recorder's perspective

Whilst reviewing the content of this atlas a key Shropshire recorder submitted this wonderful summary that I felt had to be included as a footnote which I feel sums up why we all do what we do when we head out into the great British countryside to pursue our love of natural history. It is something the politicians, the developers, and most of the public will never understand or appreciate and therefore it is something I feel we must hold dear to our hearts. Something we must cherish, and something ultimately we must fight for and protect.

'I regret that I do not have a vast store of anecdotes with which to flood the atlas. Basically I went out, looked, swept, beat, and usually failed to find anything. I have searched forget-me-not, woundwort, white dead-nettle, cleavers, birch, gorse, hawthorn, etc mostly in vain. I even thought I had found some cow-wheat so scrambled around in the ground litter only to get a thorn painfully stuck in my finger – and it turned out not to be cow-wheat anyway. Am I bitter? No. Am I disillusioned? No. I had a wonderful time trying to find these little blighters. It got me out two or three times a week and I visited all sort of places, many of which I would not have dreamt of going to but for that 'blank' tetrad on the map. I also met many people who, when I explained what I was looking for either stared at me blankly or said 'I've seen lots of them'. Perhaps they should have shown me where!

At the end of the exercise I have decided the best way to find shieldbugs is not to look for them. They will find you!'

Plant species mentioned in the text

Acer campestre field maple

Acer pseudoplatanus sycamore

Alnus glutinosa alder

Armoracia rusticana horse-radish

Ballota nigra black horehound

Brassica napus oil-seed Rape

Brassica oleracea cabbage

Brassica oleracea cultivar broccoli

Calluna vulgaris heather

Castanea sativa sweet chestnut

Chamaecyparis lawsoniana Lawson's cypress

Chamerion angustifolium rosebay willowherb

Cirsium arvense creeping thistle

Cirsium eriophorum woolly thistle

Corylus avellana hazel

Crataegus monogyna hawthorn

Cydonia oblonga quince

Cytisus scoparius broom

Epilobium hirsutum great willowherb

Epilobium palustre marsh willowherb

Erodium cicutarium common stork's-bill

Euphorbia amygdaloides wood spurge

Fraxinus excelsior ash

Galium aparine cleavers

Hedera helix ivy

Heracleum sphondylium hogweed

Ilex aquifolium holly

Impatiens glandulifera Himalayan balsam

Lamium album white dead-nettle

Lavandula angustifolia lavender

Leontodon hispidus rough hawkbit

Medicago lupulina black medick

Melampyrum pratense cow-wheat

Morus spp. mulberry

Myosotis spp. forget-me-nots

Origanum majorana marjoram

Phragmites australis common reed

Picea abies Norway spruce

Prunus spinosa blackthorn

Pseudotsuga menziesii Douglas fir

Quercus spp. oak

Raphanus sativus radish

Rubus fruticosa agg. bramble

Rumex obtusifolius broad-leaved dock

Salix spp. sallow

Sorbus spp. whitebeam

Sorbus aucuparia rowan

Stachys sylvatica hedge woundwort

Thuja plicata western red cedar

Ulex europaeus common gorse

Ulex gallii western gorse

Ulmus glabra wych elm

Urtica dioica nettle

Viola spp. violet

References

Barnard, P.C. 2011. *The Royal Entomological Society Book of British Insects*. Wiley-Blackwell, Chichester.

Curran, A. 2011. Worcestershire Record No.30, April 2011. Box Bug *Gonocerus acuteangulatus* in Edgbaston (Page 23).

Evans, M and Edmondson, R. 2005. *A Photographic Guide to the Shieldbugs and Squashbugs of the British Isles*. WGUK.

Fowler, 2012. Shropshire Entomology Newsletter – April 2012 (No.5). *Welcome to Shropshire – the Juniper Shieldbug new to Shropshire* (Pages 8-9).

Jones, N. 2010. Shropshire Invertebrates Group – Annual Report 2010 (Page 24).

Judd, S (ed). 2006. Liverpool Museum Invertebrate Survey at Llanymynech Heritage Area. Unpublished report for Shropshire County Council.

Hawkins, R. D. 2003. *Shieldbugs of Surrey*. Surrey Wildlife Trust, Woking.

McGee, K. 2007. Wyre Forest Study Group Review. Entomological Records of Note from Wyre Forest, 2007 (Page 16).

Meiklejohn, J. 2011. Worcestershire Record No.30, April 2011. *Striking Red and Black Bugs (Hemiptera – Heteroptera) in Worcestershire* (Pages 23-24).

Saruham, I, Tuncer, C. and Akça, I. 2010. *Zemdirbyste-Agriculture* Vol **97**(1) (Pages 55-60).

Southampton Natural History Society, 2007. *Shieldbugs of Southampton*. unpublished PDF document.

Unwin, D. 2001. A Key to the Families of British Bugs (Insecta, Hemiptera) *Field Studies*, **10**: 1-15. AIDGAP. Field Studies Council, Shrewsbury

Websites

British Bugs – www.britishbugs.org.uk

The Global Biodiversity Information Facility – www.gbis.org

The MBN Gateway – www.data.mbn.org.uk

Royal Horticultural Society – www.rhs.org.uk